Chile

A Requisite Travel Guide

Jeff J Scoop

Table of content

Fruit Market in Chile

Chapter 1

Overview of Chile

In the enormous and stunning nation of Chile, nature displays her magnificence in every part of the country. Nestled near the western border of South America, Chile is a region of dramatic contrasts and incomparable beauty. From the towering Andes Mountains in the east to the enormous Pacific Ocean in the west, this elongated country runs over 4,300 kilometers, making it one of the longest north-south nations on Earth.

Geographically, Chile provides a diversified scenery that would fascinate any tourist. To the north is the dry and surreal Atacama Desert, renowned as the driest desert on earth. Its unusual salt flats, lunar-like valleys, and heavenly astronomy chances have fascinated travelers and stargazers alike for decades. Moving southwards, one reaches the rich Central Valley, an agricultural heartland filled with vineyards, orchards, and farms, which has supported Chile's renowned wine industry.

The beautiful Lake District unfolds as you go farther south, marked by shimmering lakes, lush woods, and snow-capped peaks. This region shows Chile's natural beauty at its best, enticing tourists to explore its national parks, engage in outdoor sports, and immerse in the native Mapuche culture, the indigenous people of the area.

As we journey further deeper into Chile's harsh terrain, Patagonia opens before our eyes. A nation of windswept plains, freezing glaciers, and towering fjords, it leaves visitors awestruck by the sheer majesty of nature's creation. Patagonia's Torres del Paine National Park, a UNESCO Biosphere Reserve, draws hikers and nature lovers with its rugged peaks, blue lakes, and unspoiled wilderness.

But Chile's fascination goes beyond its awe-inspiring vistas. The country's history is interlaced with stories of ancient civilizations, colonial conquests, and a battle for freedom. Long before the advent of European colonization, indigenous tribes, such as the Mapuche, Aymara, and Rapa Nui, called this territory home. Their rich cultural history survives, creating the character of contemporary Chile.

In the 16th century, Spanish conquistadors set foot on Chilean territory, commencing a phase of colonization that stretched three centuries. The vestiges of colonial architecture may still be seen in picturesque towns and cities, like Valparaiso, where vivid-colored buildings tumble down slopes and labyrinthine lanes reveal artistic treasures.

The fight for Chile's independence culminated in the early 19th century, headed by courageous patriots like Bernardo O'Higgins and José de San Martín. The Battle of Maipú in 1818 heralded the birth of the Chilean nation, and since then, the country has evolved with a spirit of tenacity and resolve.

Chilean culture is a mesmerizing fabric, intertwined with a love for arts, literature, and music. The great poet Pablo Neruda, a Nobel winner, continues to inspire with his lyrics that exalt love, nature, and the human experience. In busy city streets and charming hamlet squares, you'll discover vivid murals representing tales of the past and ideas for the future.

The Chilean people, noted for their great friendliness, greet tourists with open arms. Sharing a traditional asado, a delectable barbeque, or partaking in a vibrant cueca dance, the national folk dance, are experiences that establish bonds and produce great memories.

From ancient customs to contemporary metropolises, Chile is a country of contrasts, continually growing while cherishing its legacy. With a unique combination of natural beauties, rich history, lively culture, and kind people, this lovely region begs tourists to embark on a voyage of exploration, discovery, and awe-inspiring adventures. The heart of Chile pulsates with a pulse that resonates profoundly with those who dare to unearth its riches, leaving an unforgettable impact on their spirits for years to come.

Chapter 2

Top Tourist Destinations

Embark on a fascinating tour through Chile's most compelling sites, where nature's beauties and cultural pearls merge to create a unique travel experience.

First on your must-visit list is Santiago, the pulsing heart of Chile. Nestled in a valley encircled by the Andes, this busy town integrates modernism with a strong respect for its ancient origins. Stroll around the colorful streets, and you'll discover the rich tapestry of Santiago's districts, each providing its special character. From the hippie ambiance of Bellavista to the trendy stores of Lastarria, every corner has a tale waiting to be told.

A short trip from Santiago brings you to the scenic Valparaiso, an artistic utopia where creativity knows no limitations. Ascend its labyrinthine slopes decorated with vividly painted cottages, and you'll understand why this UNESCO World Heritage Site has inspired innumerable painters, authors, and dreamers over the years. Get lost in the graffiti-covered lanes that emanate a feeling of playfulness and rebellion, and don't forget to take a trip on one of the classic funiculars that highlight beautiful views of the Pacific Ocean.

For an experience with ethereal beauty, go north to the Atacama Desert, an exotic region that will make you feel like you've walked into another planet. As the world's driest desert, the Atacama provides bizarre landscapes with immense salt flats, towering dunes, and spectacular rock formations. As night sets, you'll be amazed by the view of the cleanest sky possible, where stars appear to dance in unison with the cosmos.

On the southernmost point of Chile sits Patagonia, an area famous for awe-inspiring wildness. Brace yourself for encounters with huge glaciers, including the famed Perito Moreno Glacier, where large pieces of ice calve into the blue seas below. Explore the famed Torres del Paine National Park, where magnificent granite spires pierce the sky, and pure lakes reflect the magnificence of the surrounding nature. Patagonia's raw and untamed beauty will ignite your soul and leave an unforgettable impact on your spirit.

But the marvels of Chile do not stop there. Journey to the magical Easter Island, or Rapa Nui, where enormous stone moai sculptures calmly watch over the land. Unravel the secrets of an ancient society, and immerse yourself in the island's Polynesian history. Here, traditions and tales are alive, lending a layer of magic to this distant and mysterious sanctuary.

As you tour Chile's varied geography, you'll meet hospitable inhabitants who represent the spirit of Chilean hospitality. Share in their delight at exuberant fiestas, experience the flavors of traditional food and embrace the rhythms of cueca dance that honor the soul of this amazing country.

In every area of Chile, from the busy streets to the distant wilderness, you'll encounter a blend of natural beauty, cultural depth, and warm-hearted people that will leave you in amazement and hungry for more. Let your senses be your guide as you explore these must-visit destinations because Chile's identity rests not only in what you see but also in how it makes you feel a country where adventure, wonder, and discovery await at every turn.

Chapter 3

Activities and Adventures

Prepare to immerse yourself in a symphony of amazing outdoor experiences that Chile provides to adventurous spirits seeking an intimate touch with nature's greatest treasures.

For those who want the excitement of conquering untamed landscapes, Chile's numerous terrains call you to go on epic excursions that will leave tracks on your heart. Patagonia's Torres del Paine National Park, a paradise for hikers, includes the classic "W" journey, called for its form that brings you through awe-inspiring valleys, through beautiful lakes, and up close to the iconic granite towers that stand tall like guardians of this pure environment.

But the escapades don't stop there. The Atacama Desert, however, parched, contains beautiful scenery suited for hiking aficionados. Explore the Moon Valley, where the salt sculptures and dunes mirror the surface of the moon, or travel to the Tatio Geysers, where the early morning mist gives way to the hypnotic sight of geysers spouting steam into the sky.

In the winter months, Chile's ski resorts become a wonderland for snow enthusiasts. Among the most recognized is Valle Nevado, whose world-class slopes and powder-filled terrain draw skiers and snowboarders from every part of the globe. The Andes Mountains offer a stunning background as you cut your way down the slopes, experiencing the adrenaline rush that only the mountains can deliver.

But if your heart yearns for a more laid-back excursion, Chile's wine tours will please your senses. Journey through the verdant Central Valley, where vines spread to the horizon, and you'll find yourself in the center of one of South America's most major wine-producing areas. Sip on the beautiful tastes of Chilean Cabernet Sauvignon, Carmenere, and Sauvignon Blanc, while learning about the winemaking process from devoted vintners who have honed their art for generations.

Venture to the distant reaches of Chile to enjoy wildlife viewing like never before. The oceans of Chiloé Island and the Chonos Archipelago provide a natural haven for marine species, from playful sea lions to magnificent blue whales. Keep your eyes open for the lovely sight of dolphins dancing in the surf as you sail through these beautiful seas.

Chile's wildness teems with distinctive animals, like the famed guanacos that wander the Patagonian steppe, and the elusive pumas that quietly traverse the highlands. Birdwatchers will be in delight when they witness bright flamingos on the Atacama salt flats or get a glimpse of the vivid Andean condor flying high above the mountains.

No, whatever your outdoor passion, Chile has something spectacular to offer. It's a country where the spirit of adventure is woven into the fabric of the terrain, and where your greatest aspirations are waiting to be realized. Whether you want the excitement of climbing peaks, the calm of drinking wine amid vineyards, or the delight of discovering wild species in their natural habitats, Chile's outdoor paradise welcomes you to experience the remarkable and redefines the meaning of travel.

Chapter 4

Local Cuisine and Dining

Prepare your taste buds for a delectable gourmet adventure as we dig into the rich tapestry of Chilean cuisine, where traditional dishes, regional specialties, and renowned restaurants meet to create a feast for the senses.

At the core of Chile's culinary legacy is the modest empanada, a cherished pastry stuffed with an assortment of tasty ingredients. Sink your teeth into a typical empanada de pino, loaded with a delicious blend of minced beef, onions, olives, and boiled eggs, embodying the essence of Chilean tastes in every mouthful. As you explore the nation, you'll meet regional varieties that illustrate the range of fillings, from seafood in coastal areas to cheese and maize in the Andean communities.

To completely immerse yourself in the spirit of Chilean cuisine, indulge in a hearty bowl of cazuela, a soothing stew that warms the heart and feeds the soul. With a basis of soft beef or chicken, this classic meal boasts an assortment of vegetables including potatoes, pumpkin, corn, and carrots, all boiled together in a fragrant broth that encapsulates the spirit of home-cooked comfort.

Chile's coastal towns provide a variety of seafood specialties, and a highlight not to be missed is the famed Chilean ceviche. Bursting with fresh aromas, this citrus-marinated meal blends a variety of fish and shellfish, topped with onions, cilantro, and a dash of scorching heat to stimulate the taste senses. Savor each spicy mouthful as the tastes take you to the sun-kissed beaches of the Pacific Ocean.

As you journey to the scenic valleys of central Chile, make sure to revel in the thrill of pastel de choclo, a classic maize pie that has adorned Chilean tables for centuries. With a golden crust made from sweet corn, this delicious pleasure is packed with ground beef, chicken, olives, raisins, and a hard-boiled egg surprise in the middle. It's a perfect combination of tastes that captures the essence of Chile's agricultural history.

Venturing farther south, the food takes on a more rustic character, with the introduction of curanto, a traditional meal cooked in a hole in the ground. This gastronomic gem contains an assortment of meats, fish, potatoes, and vegetables, all slow-cooked to perfection with hot stones and fragrant leaves, giving a smokey fragrance that stimulates the senses.

In the metropolitan centers of Santiago and Valparaiso, a dynamic cuisine scene awaits you, where brilliant chefs merge classic dishes with a modern flare. Upscale restaurants and hidden treasures alike provide a blend of flavors that respect Chilean culinary heritage while embracing global influences. From street cuisine pleasures like chorrillanas, a robust combination of French fries, beef, eggs, and onions, to gourmet meals like Patagonian lamb or

Araucanía mushrooms, these urban oasis accommodate to every palette and gastronomic curiosity.

And let's not forget the pleasure of Chile's burgeoning wine industry. As you explore the Central Valley's vineyards, you'll have the opportunity to enjoy exceptional wine pairings that raise the dining experience to new heights. With vineyards producing world-renowned varietals, such as Carmenere and Cabernet Sauvignon, each taste is a testament to Chile's viticultural greatness.

In every region of Chile, from the busy metropolis to the rural villages, the food serves as a reflection of the country's history, geography, and cultural legacy. Savoring traditional meals, experiencing regional specialties, and eating at prominent restaurants will take you on a gastronomic trip that celebrates the variety and depth of Chilean cuisine, leaving you with treasured memories and a greater respect for the art of food.

Chapter 5

Practical Travel Information

Embarking on a vacation to Chile is a lovely notion, and to guarantee a flawless and enjoyable trip, it's vital to be well-informed about visa requirements, currency, transportation alternatives, safety precautions, and more.

Visa Requirements: Chile cordially welcomes tourists from many countries, enabling them to enter visa-free for short visits. Citizens of nations including the United States, Canada, the European Union, Australia, and many more may normally remain in Chile for up to 90 days without a visa. However, it is always essential to verify the current visa restrictions with the Chilean consulate or embassy in your own country before flying.

Currency & Money Matters: The Chilean Peso (CLP) is the official currency, and you'll find that most locations prefer cash payments, particularly in smaller towns and local enterprises. ATMs are prevalent in cities, and major credit cards are frequently accepted at hotels, restaurants, and bigger businesses. However, it's advisable to carry some cash for remote locations and smaller enterprises.

Transportation Options: Chile features a well-connected transportation network, making it easier for tourists to explore the nation. In major hubs like Santiago, you'll discover an efficient subway system, buses, and taxis to explore the city. For lengthier travels between cities, domestic planes provide a time-efficient choice. Additionally, Chile's wide bus network covers many places, making it a popular option among budget-conscious visitors who prefer to take in stunning surroundings along the journey.

Safety Tips: Chile is a generally safe country for tourists, but it's always important to take care, as you would on any foreign trip. Keep your valuables protected and avoid exhibiting them in busy situations. In bigger cities, stay careful of pickpockets in tourist destinations. When exploring nature's treasures, particularly in distant places, it's wise to obtain information from local authorities regarding weather conditions and possible threats.

Health and immunizations: Before coming to Chile, it's important to speak with a healthcare expert to ensure you are up-to-date with regular immunizations. Depending on your itinerary and medical history, extra vaccines or preventative measures can be required. Also, don't forget to obtain travel health insurance to defend against unforeseen medical bills.

Language & Communication: The official language of Chile is Spanish, and although English is spoken in tourist regions and major towns, it's good to know some basic Spanish phrases to enrich your travel experience and connect with locals. Chileans are typically courteous and appreciative of attempts to speak their language.

Cultural Sensitivity: Chileans take pleasure in their rich cultural past, thus it's necessary to respect local customs and traditions. Greetings are generally with a handshake, and it's courteous to greet them using their titles (Mr. or Mrs.) until encouraged to use their name. Additionally, wearing modest clothing while visiting religious places or traditional villages is considered polite.

Climate & Packing Essentials: Chile's location means it experiences a range of temperatures, from the parched Atacama Desert to the frigid Patagonian area. Pack appropriately, and consider layers to adjust to changing climates. Sunscreen, a hat, and sunglasses are must-haves since the sun can be harsh in many regions of the nation.

By familiarizing yourself with these practicalities, you're well-equipped to begin on an unforgettable trip through the beautiful landscapes and rich culture of Chile, where each moment will be an experience filled with wonder and discovery.

Chapter 6

Accommodation Options

When it comes to housing choices in Chile, tourists are spoiled for choice, with a vast assortment of hotels, hostels, and unique stays that suit every taste and budget. From opulent getaways to charming boutique hostels and unique accommodations, Chile provides a broad choice of housing options that enhance your adventure to new heights.

Luxurious Retreats: For those seeking extravagance and comfort, Chile provides a range of world-class hotels and resorts that radiate elegance and refinement. In Santiago, the capital city, you'll discover prominent 5-star hotels set amid the busy metropolis, providing immaculate service, rich facilities, and breathtaking city views. In the wine districts of Colchagua and Casablanca, opulent vineyard retreats give an escape into peace, where visitors may enjoy great wines, spa treatments, and gourmet dining experiences.

Charming Boutique Hotels: Chile is ornamented with a selection of boutique hotels, each with its particular character and charm. In the picturesque port city of Valparaiso, you may discover tiny boutique hotels set on the hills, affording panoramic perspectives of the colorful residences and the great Pacific Ocean. In the Lake District, you'll be delighted by quaint cottages nestled away in the middle of lush woods and scenic lakes, encouraging tourists to reconnect with nature and relax in tranquil settings.

Cozy Hostels: For budget-conscious tourists, Chile's hostels provide a warm and welcoming environment, excellent for meeting new friends and swapping travel tales. In Santiago and other major areas, bustling hostels welcome travelers and lone explorers, offering dormitory-style lodgings and public spaces that encourage a feeling of solidarity. The coastal cities of

Valparaiso and Viña del Mar offer hostels with ocean views, where you may wake up to the sound of waves slamming against the beach.

Eco-Lodges and Unique Stays: Chile's dedication to sustainability is evident in the establishment of eco-lodges and unique stays that integrate with the natural surroundings. In the Atacama Desert, you'll encounter eco-friendly hotels that mix effortlessly with the desert nature, creating a tranquil sanctuary in the middle of the huge dunes and salt flats. In the magical Chiloé Island, immerse yourself in traditional palafitos, stilt dwellings above water, where the calming sound of the sea lulls you into a state of serenity.

Glamping Experiences: For explorers wanting a touch of elegance in the woods, glamping (glamorous camping) is a popular alternative in Chile. Picture yourself in a sumptuous tent among the breathtaking landscapes of Patagonia, where you can admire the beauty of nature while enjoying the comfort of soft bedding and sophisticated furniture. Glamping sites may also be found in the Lake District, providing a unique blend of outdoor adventure and sophisticated comfort.

Off-the-Grid resorts: In distant parts of Chile, off-the-grid resorts encourage guests to disconnect from the modern world and immerse themselves in pure natural environments. Whether it's an isolated cabin in the Andes or a lonely lodge in the center of Patagonia's wildness, these tranquil getaways give an opportunity to relax, rejuvenate, and enjoy the beauty of simplicity.

Whichever hotel choice you pick, Chile guarantees to give you a wonderful and fulfilling visit. From the heights of luxury to the warmth of hostels and the charm of unique accommodations, the vast choice of accommodation options in Chile assures that every traveler's trip is a reflection of their distinct sense of adventure.

Chapter 7

Cultural Experiences

Dive into the captivating tapestry of Chilean cultural heritage, where vibrant festivals, expressive art, soul-stirring music, and time-honored traditions come together to create a rich and immersive experience that lingers in your heart and soul.

Festivals:
Chile's calendar is brimming with colorful festivals, each celebrating a unique aspect of the nation's history, culture, and spirituality. One of the most famous is La Tirana Festival, held in the small town of La Tirana in northern Chile. This mesmerizing celebration pays homage to the Virgen del Carmen, drawing thousands of pilgrims and spectators to witness vibrant dances, elaborate costumes, and an infectious atmosphere of joy and devotion.

In Chiloé Island, the Chiloé Festival takes center stage, showcasing the island's cultural identity through traditional dances, music, and culinary delights. The sight of costumed dancers gracefully moving to the rhythm of lively music is a spectacle that transports you back in time and immerses you in the island's enchanting folklore.

Art and Crafts:
Chile's art scene is a melting pot of creativity and expression, drawing inspiration from its diverse landscapes and cultural heritage. Throughout the country, you'll find art galleries and craft markets that showcase the talent of local artisans. From intricately woven textiles to intricately carved woodwork and vibrant paintings, Chilean art is a reflection of the nation's history, identity, and deep connection to nature.

In the artistic haven of Valparaiso, the city itself becomes an open-air gallery, where every wall is a canvas for colorful murals that narrate stories of the past and visions for the future. Stroll through Valparaiso's winding streets, and you'll discover a living canvas that encapsulates the spirit of Chilean creativity and artistic expression.

Music and Dance:
Music and dance are an integral part of Chilean culture, capturing the soul and spirit of the nation's people. The national dance, cueca, is a lively and spirited performance that symbolizes courtship and love. The dance's graceful movements, accompanied by the harmonious melodies of guitar and accordion, invite everyone to join in the celebration.

Chile's vibrant music scene spans various genres, from folk music that celebrates rural traditions to the passionate sounds of Nueva Canción Chilena, a movement that emerged during the country's political upheavals, expressing resistance and hope through song. Discover talented musicians performing in Santiago's intimate venues or experience impromptu street performances that fill the air with the rhythm of Chilean melodies.

Local Traditions:
Chile's local traditions are deeply rooted in its indigenous heritage and the influences of Spanish colonization. One such tradition is the feast of the Andean crossing, celebrated by the Mapuche people, where they give thanks for the abundance of the land and seek blessings for the journey ahead. The ceremony blends ancient rituals with Christian elements, creating a harmonious fusion of beliefs.

Another cherished tradition is the rodeo, a sport that honors Chile's rural heritage and skilled horsemanship. Rodeos bring together riders to showcase their equestrian prowess, while spectators cheer on in an atmosphere of camaraderie and pride.

In the coastal regions, fishing communities celebrate the blessing of the sea with the Festival of the Virgin of Carmel. Colorful processions, boat parades, and feasts of freshly caught seafood pay homage to the sea's bounty and the fishermen's livelihood.

Immersing in Chile's cultural heritage allows you to connect with the soul of the nation, to understand its history, and to celebrate the creativity, spirit, and traditions of its people. From the joyous festivities to the expressive arts, the captivating music to the cherished local customs, Chile's cultural tapestry weaves a story of identity and pride, inviting you to embrace the essence of this remarkable land and its warm-hearted people.

Chapter 8

Travel Tips and Recommendations

Embarking on a tour across the magnificent landscapes of Chile is a fascinating idea, and to ensure your vacation is seamless and pleasurable, consider these useful recommendations that go beyond the standard travel advice.

Embrace the Chilean Pace: In Chile, time flows at its best, so embrace the native mentality and allow yourself to relish every minute. Don't hurry from one site to the next; instead, linger in scenic squares, engage in talks with people, and allow the beauty of the surroundings to sink into your spirit.

Sip & Savor: Chile is a haven for foodies and wine connoisseurs, so make sure to sample the local specialties and wines. Explore busy food markets for genuine snacks, drink on velvety reds in vineyard getaways, and experience the particular flavors of each location. Let your taste buds be your guide, and you'll find a gourmet trip like no other.

Connect with Locals: Chileans are kind and inviting, and embracing their culture provides a route to a richer travel experience. Engage with people, learn some basic Spanish words, and engage in their rituals and traditions. By building ties with the people, you'll acquire insights into their way of life and create amazing experiences.

Layer Up for Varied temperatures: Chile's diversified topography means you'll experience a variety of temperatures, from desert heat to frigid mountain air. Pack adaptable apparel, including layers, to adjust to changing weather conditions. A sun hat and sunscreen are needed to defend against the intense rays of the sun, wherever your travel takes you.

Seek Out Off-the-Beaten-Path Treasures: While popular places like Santiago and Patagonia are must-visit sites, try exploring lesser-known wonders. Venture to secluded towns, distant national parks, and tranquil islands to unearth the country's hidden beauty and enjoy unique experiences that few tourists have the chance to see.

Capture Moments, Not Just Images: While it's normal to want to chronicle your adventure with images, remember to put the camera down at times and truly immerse yourself in the experience. Let the beauty of the surroundings wash over you, capture mental pictures of rare moments, and appreciate the memories that stay in your heart.

Respect Nature and Wildlife: Chile's wilderness is a treasure mine of species, therefore practice responsible travel to preserve its beauty. Follow established pathways, abstain from disturbing animals, and leave no record of your presence. By protecting the natural environment, you guarantee that future generations may likewise relish in its grandeur.

Embrace serendipity: While it's wonderful to have an agenda, make space for serendipity in your trips. Allow yourself to stray off the beaten route, pursue unforeseen possibilities, and say yes to unexpected experiences. Some of the most treasured experiences stem from unexpected meetings and unforeseen diversions.

In essence, a seamless and delightful visit to Chile is not only about checking off sights but about immersing oneself in the heart and spirit of this magnificent place. Embrace the pace, connect with the people, appreciate the delicacies, and let the spirit of Chile's various landscapes and warm-hearted culture kindle a spark of amazement within you, permanently transforming the way you view the world.

Printed in the USA
CPSIA information can be obtained
at www.ICGtesting.com
LVHW021051131023
761026LV00016B/271